DRUM MAKING

Mastering the Art of Drum Making: Expert Techniques, Materials, and Designs for Crafting Authentic, Handmade Drums with Precision and Passion

Kenyetta Miltons

Table Of Contents

CHAPTER ONE

Drum Making

Making drums is a craft that goes beyond simple fabrication; it explores the core of human rhythm, craftsmanship, and cultural expression. Drums have been used in ceremonies, rituals, and daily life for generations, across continents. Every instrument, from the Native American powwow drum to the African djembe, conveys a tale of custom, spirituality, and community in addition to a rhythm.

Comprehending The Craft Of Drum Making

It takes an appreciation of the complex fusion of talent, tradition, and devotion required in the process to really understand drum manufacture. Making a drum is more than just putting parts together; it's a way to connect with nature by using the earth's rhythms and the wisdom of the past.

The Artisanship of Drum Crafting: Fundamentally, drum crafting is an expression of human resourcefulness and inventiveness. Craftspeople meticulously choose materials like metal, wood, and leather, each one selected for its distinct aesthetic and acoustic characteristics. Every stage, from stretching the skin to forming the drum frame, calls for patience and accuracy that has been developed over decades of use.

The Spiritual Aspect: A drum has spiritual significance in many cultures beyond its material appearance. Drums are used by indigenous peoples all throughout the world as a means of asking for favors, communicating with the divine, and offering prayers. The drum's steady pulse unites the individual with communal awareness, creating a soundscape that is beyond boundaries and language.

The Legacy of Tradition: The craft of drumming serves as a monument to the lasting strength of tradition in a world that is changing quickly. A living link to history that reverberates in the present, each drum represents a transmission of centuries of wisdom and skill from master to student. Every drum, whether it is made in a busy city or a far-off village, conveys a tale of resiliency and continuity, safeguarding cultural legacy for the next generations.

The Value Of Making Drums In Different Cultures

Drums are an integral part of community life in many different cultures and environments, acting as markers of celebration, solidarity, and identity. Beyond the realm of musical performance, the significance of drum creation is evident in the melancholy melodies of Native American powwows and the throbbing rhythms of West African drum circles.

Ritual & Ceremony: Drums are integral to many cultures' rituals and ceremonies, which commemorate significant life events like marriages, births, and deaths. The booming sound of the drum calls everyone together for a time of communal prayer, dancing, and introspection. Drums give a holy soundtrack to life's most meaningful events, whether they are used to invoke ancestral spirits or celebrate natural cycles.

Fundamentally, drumming creates a sense of togetherness and connection that cuts over boundaries of language and culture. People from various walks of life gather in drum circles all over the world to enjoy the joys of song and rhythm, forming connections that cross social boundaries and promote understanding.

Drumming fosters empathy, collaboration, and solidarity via the universal language of music, cultivating a sense of global belonging.

Cultural Identity and Resilience: Drumming is a potent weapon of cultural resistance and resilience for marginalized populations. Drums offer a physical connection to ancestry in the face of colonialism, injustice, and cultural erasure, reclaiming space and demanding the right to cultural self-determination. Communities are empowered to proudly exhibit their identity and heritage via drum manufacturing, whether it is by restoring old methods or creating new avenues for cultural expression.

To sum up, creating drums is a living heritage that captures the essence of mankind itself, not merely a craft. Drum creation, with its unique combination of artistry, spirituality, and cultural importance, has the power to uplift people's lives and create links between generations and continents.

 Let us keep in mind the eternal knowledge contained in the drum's rhythmic heartbeat, which serves as a reminder that some traditions are still valuable in today's world of rapid change.

CHAPTER TWO

Beginning

Making your own drums from scratch is a rewarding musical and artistic endeavor. The technique provides a combination of creativity, accuracy, and cultural history, regardless of your level of experience as an artisan or your curiosity. It's crucial to set the foundation for your project before delving into the nuances of drum building. This entails assembling the relevant supplies, choosing the perfect wood, and becoming acquainted with the instruments needed for the job. You may create a drum that not only has a rhythmic resonance but also expresses your own style and workmanship if you put in the necessary effort and enthusiasm.

Materials Required to Make a Drum

The components needed to create a drum set are the same as those needed to create a musical masterpiece. Every part is essential to the drum's endurance, sound quality, and visual appeal. The following is a detailed inventory of everything you will require to start manufacturing drums:

1. Wood: The main component of the drum shell, the choice of wood has a big effect on the resonance and tone of the instrument. Popular options include mahogany, birch, oak, and maple; each has unique qualities that affect the final sound.

2. Drum Hoops: Also referred to as rims or rings, these components give the drumhead tension and structural support. Wood or metal may be used to create them, according to your taste and preferred look.

3. Drumhead: The thin membrane covering the drum shell that makes sound when struck is called the drumhead. A variety of materials, including traditional animal skins like goat or calfskin and synthetic materials like Mylar, may be used to provide distinct tonal characteristics for the drum.

4. Adhesives: To firmly join the parts of the drum shell and fasten the drumhead to the frame, high-quality glue or adhesive is required. Select an adhesive that is sturdy enough to endure the strain and pressure that comes with playing.

5. Hardware is what's utilized to put the drum together and change its tension. It consists of bolts, screws, and lugs. Select gear that is robust enough to endure repeated tweaking and playing.

6. Finishing Materials: Sealants, varnishes, and stains give your drum the last touch while strengthening its aesthetic appeal and shielding it from the elements. Take into account your drum's

aesthetics and select finishing materials that go well with its style.

7. Decorative Accents: You may give your instrument a personalized touch and a one-of-a-kind look by adding optional decorations like drum wraps, inlays, or original artwork. When you add ornamental elements to your drum, don't be afraid to express your creativity.

8. Safety Equipment: Although not specifically included in the drum, protective equipment including dust masks, goggles, and gloves is crucial for your own protection during building. Make sure you have all the safety gear required to avoid mishaps and injury.

After assembling these supplies, you'll be ready to start building drums with confidence and excitement. The tone, look, and overall quality of the instrument are greatly influenced by each component, so make thoughtful selections and spend money on premium materials that match your expectations for the final result.

Selecting The Proper Wood

When making drums, choosing the right wood is an important choice that affects the aesthetics, resonance, and sound of the finished product. With so many alternatives available, each with distinct qualities and tones, selecting the correct wood takes careful thought and a clear grasp of what you want to achieve. This thorough guide will assist you in navigating the world of drum wood selection:

1. Maple: Maple is a well-liked material for drum shells because of its warm resonance and well-balanced tonal qualities. Its smooth texture and dense grain structure give it a rich, full-bodied sound with distinct highs, mids, and lows.

Drummers of all genres prefer maple drums because of their clarity and versatility.

2. Birch: Drummers looking for clarity and projection love birch because of its bright, articulate sound and pronounced attack. Birch shells are perfect for live performances and recording environments where the definition is crucial because they produce a focused, punchy sound with improved presence and projection.

3. Oak: valued for its robustness and longevity, oak gives drums a bold, powerful sound with distinct lows and a powerful midrange punch. Heavy hitters and genres like rock, metal, and marching bands that require volume and projection are a good fit for oak shells.

4. Respected for its deep harmonic range and warm, resonant tone, mahogany is a traditional material for drum shells, especially in jazz, blues, and retro-inspired music. With a focus on the low

end, mahogany drums have a smooth, rounded sound that gives each note warmth and depth.

5. Cherry: prized for its lively grain patterns and gentle, sweet tone, cherry wood creates drums with a well-balanced, melodic sound that works well in a variety of musical contexts. Cherry shells can be used in a variety of playing styles and genres because of their unique combination of warmth, clarity, and sustain.

6. Walnut: valued for its distinct grain patterns and earthy, dark tone, walnut produces warm, resonant drums with a noticeable low-end response. Rich, full-bodied, and decaying smoothly, walnut shells are perfect for genres like blues, jazz, and fusion that call for warmth and depth.

7. Exotic Woods: Exotic woods like Purpleheart, padauk, and bubinga provide interesting choices for those looking for distinctive aesthetics and tonal qualities. These woods stand out from more

conventional options thanks to their remarkable sonic profiles, vivid colors, and eye-catching grain patterns.

Think about things like playing style, tone preferences, and aesthetics when choosing wood for your drum. Trying out various wood kinds and combinations can yield fascinating results and assist you in creating a drum that is precisely in line with your style of music.

Instruments Needed to Make Drums

When building a drum from the ground up, a wide range of tools are needed, each with a distinct function. Having the proper tools on hand is crucial for attaining accuracy, effectiveness, and superior quality in your work, from forming the drum shell to putting together hardware and fastening the drumhead. The following is a detailed inventory of all the tools needed to make drums:

1. Tools for Woodworking:

• Band Saw: This tool is used to cut large pieces of wood into drum shell blanks.

• Table Saw: Perfect for cross-cutting and ripping wood to the right size for different drum parts.

• Router: A necessary tool for forming snare beds, bearing edges, and other fine details on the drum shell.

• Drill Press: Allows for accurate drilling of holes for venting and hardware attachment.

• Lathe: For turning drum shells that are cylindrical and producing even, smooth surfaces.

2. Hand Instruments:

• Chisels: These are necessary for manually carving the drum shell's snare beds, bearing edges, and other fine details.

• Files and Rasps: These tools are useful for smoothing and shaping wood surfaces, especially in tight spaces.

• Clamps: Crucial for guaranteeing strong, tight bonds during glue-up and assembly, they secure drum components.

• Sanding Tools: For smoothing and polishing wood surfaces, use orbital sanders, sandpaper, and sanding blocks.

3. Tools for Measuring and Marking:

• Tape Measure: Essential for taking accurate measurements of drum components and dimensions.

• Square: Used for ensuring straight, square cuts and proper alignment during assembly.

• Calipers: Ideal for measuring precise dimensions and tolerances, particularly for bearing edges and hardware placement.

• Marking Gauge: Enables accurate marking of reference lines and dimensions on wood surfaces.

4. Finishing Tools:

• Paint Brushes/Rollers: Used for applying stains, varnishes, and sealants to the drum shell and hardware.

• Spray Gun: Ideal for applying smooth, even coats of paint or lacquer to larger drum surfaces.

• Polishing Pads: Used for buffing and polishing finished drum surfaces to a high gloss or satin sheen.

5. Safety Gear:

• Safety Glasses: Essential for protecting your eyes from flying debris and dust particles during cutting, shaping, and sanding.

• Dust Mask/Respirator: Helps prevent inhalation of wood dust and fumes generated during the woodworking process.

• Gloves: Provide hand protection when handling sharp tools, abrasive materials, and chemicals.

By assembling a comprehensive set of tools and equipment, you'll be well-prepared to tackle every aspect of drum-making with confidence and precision. Whether you're shaping wood, assembling hardware, or applying finishes, having the right tools at your disposal is essential for bringing your musical vision to life.

CHAPTER THREE

Crafting The Shell

Crafting the shell of a drum from scratch involves several meticulous steps, each contributing to the overall quality and resonance of the instrument. From selecting the appropriate wood to shaping and joining the shell, every aspect demands attention to detail and a deep understanding of the craft.

Preparing The Wood

The choice of wood is paramount in drum making, as it directly influences the sound and durability of the instrument. Typically, hardwoods such as maple, birch, or mahogany are preferred for their resonance and strength. Before any cutting or shaping takes place, the wood must be properly seasoned to ensure stability and prevent warping over time.

Seasoning involves drying the wood to the optimal moisture content, usually around 6-8%. This process can take several months to a year, depending on the type of wood and environmental conditions. Properly seasoned wood not only enhances the sound quality of the drum but also prevents cracks and structural issues down the line.

Once seasoned, the wood is carefully inspected for any imperfections or defects that could affect the integrity of the drum shell. Knots, splits, and irregular grain patterns are identified and either repaired or avoided altogether. This attention to detail ensures that the final product meets the highest standards of craftsmanship.

Cutting And Shaping The Shell

With the wood prepared, the next step is to cut it into the appropriate sizes and shapes for the drum shell. Precision is key here, as even minor deviations can affect the sound and aesthetics of the instrument. Drum shells are typically constructed from several plies of wood, which are cut to uniform thickness and stacked to achieve the desired depth.

Modern techniques such as CNC machining have made the cutting process more efficient and accurate, but many craftsmen still prefer to cut and shape the shells by hand. This hands-on approach allows for greater control and customization, resulting in truly unique instruments with character and soul.

Once the individual plies are cut, they are carefully shaped to form the curved profile of the drum shell. This can be done using a variety of tools, including routers, sanders, and hand planes. The goal is to create smooth, seamless joints between the plies, ensuring a solid foundation for the drum.

Joining the Shell Together

Joining the plies of the drum shell is perhaps the most critical step in the construction process. There are several methods for doing this, each with its own advantages and challenges. Traditional methods such as steam bending and gluing involve carefully shaping the plies and clamping them together until the adhesive sets.

Another popular technique is known as stave construction, where the individual plies are cut into narrow strips and glued together edge-to-edge to form the shell. This method allows for greater control over the shell's thickness and results in a distinctive segmented appearance.

Regardless of the joining method used, attention to detail is crucial to ensure a strong and stable bond between the plies. Any gaps or inconsistencies in the joints can compromise the integrity of the shell and negatively impact the sound of the drum.

In conclusion, crafting the shell of a drum from scratch is a labor-intensive process that requires patience, skill, and a deep passion for the craft. From selecting the finest wood to meticulously shaping and joining the shell, every step is essential to creating an instrument of unparalleled quality and beauty.

CHAPTER FOUR

Drumhead Selection And Preparation

Understanding Different Types Of Drumheads

When embarking on the journey of drum-making from scratch, selecting the right drumhead is paramount to achieving the desired sound and performance. Drumheads come in various materials, each offering distinct tonal qualities and durability. One of the most common materials is Mylar, a synthetic material known for its consistency and resilience. Mylar drumheads produce a bright, articulate sound, making them suitable for various musical genres ranging from rock to jazz.

For those seeking a warmer, more vintage sound, natural skin drumheads present an excellent option. Typically crafted from animal hides such as goat, calf, or buffalo, natural skin drumheads offer a rich, earthy tone that resonates beautifully across different styles of music. However, it's essential to note that natural skin drumheads require meticulous care and maintenance to retain their optimal sound quality, as they are susceptible to changes in humidity and temperature.

Additionally, specialized drumheads, such as those coated with materials like Kevlar or equipped with built-in dampening features, cater to specific preferences and playing styles. Coated drumheads offer enhanced durability and control over overtones, making them ideal for heavy hitters or those seeking a more controlled sound.

Preparing the Drumhead for Attachment

Once you've selected the appropriate drumhead for your project, proper preparation is key to ensuring a successful attachment to the drum shell. Begin by inspecting the drumhead for any defects or irregularities that may affect its performance. Check for tears, dents, or uneven stretching, as these issues can compromise the integrity of the drumhead and impact its sound quality.

Next, carefully clean the surface of the drumhead to remove any dust, debris, or residue that may have accumulated during storage or transportation. Use a soft, lint-free cloth lightly dampened with water to gently wipe away any dirt or grime, taking care not to apply excessive pressure that could damage the drumhead.

Once the drumhead is clean and free of debris, it's time to prepare it for attachment to the drum shell. If you're working with a natural skin drumhead, you may need to soak it in water for a period of time to soften the material and facilitate stretching. Be sure to follow the manufacturer's recommendations for soaking time and temperature to avoid over-soaking or damaging the drumhead.

For Mylar or coated drumheads, stretching may not be necessary, but you'll still want to ensure the drumhead is free of wrinkles or creases that could affect its performance. Gently smooth out any imperfections with your hands, taking care to maintain even tension across the surface of the drumhead.

Attaching the Drumhead to the Shell

With the drumhead properly prepared, it's time to attach it to the drum shell. Start by placing the drumhead over the top of the drum shell, ensuring that it is centered and aligned correctly. Depending on the type of drumhead and drum shell you're working with, you may need to use a hoop or tension rods to secure the drumhead in place.

If you're using a hoop, carefully position it over the edge of the drumhead and drum shell, making sure that it sits flush against the surface. Slowly tighten the tension rods in a crisscross pattern, gradually increasing the tension on the drumhead to achieve the desired pitch and tone. Take care not to over-tighten the tension rods, as this can put unnecessary strain on the drumhead and potentially cause damage.

For drums equipped with a lug system, insert the tension rods through the holes in the hoop and thread them into the lugs on the drum shell. Again, tighten the tension rods in a crisscross pattern, gradually increasing the tension until the drumhead is securely attached and tuned to your liking.

Once the drumhead is properly attached and tuned, give it a few test strikes to ensure that it's responding as expected and producing the desired sound. Make any necessary adjustments to the tension rods or tuning to achieve the perfect tone, and voila – you've successfully prepared and attached a drumhead to your custom-made drum shell, ready to unleash your musical creativity.

1. Applying Protective Coatings

When it comes to drum making, applying protective coatings is a crucial step to ensure the longevity and durability of the instrument. These coatings serve as a shield against wear and tear, moisture, and other environmental factors that could potentially damage the drum. There are several types of protective coatings available, each with its own unique properties and application methods.

Types of Protective Coatings

Shellac: Shellac is a natural resin derived from the lac bug and is often used as a protective coating for drums. It provides a glossy finish and excellent protection against moisture and scratches. Applying shellac involves using a brush or spray gun to evenly coat the surface of the drum shell. Multiple coats may be applied for added protection and a smoother finish.

Polyurethane: Polyurethane is a synthetic resin that offers superior durability and resistance to moisture, chemicals, and abrasion. It is available in both water-based and oil-based formulations, with the water-based option being more environmentally friendly. Applying polyurethane involves sanding the drum surface to ensure smoothness and then using a brush or roller to apply thin, even coats. Sanding between coats helps achieve a flawless finish.

Lacquer: Lacquer is a quick-drying, solvent-based coating that provides a high-gloss finish and excellent protection for drum shells. It is available in various colors and can be sprayed or brushed onto the drum surface. Lacquer dries rapidly, allowing for multiple coats to be applied in a short amount of time. However, proper ventilation is essential when working with lacquer due to its strong fumes.

Application Process

1. Preparation: Before applying any protective coating, it is essential to prepare the drum surface properly. This involves sanding the shell to remove any imperfections, dirt, or previous coatings. The surface should be smooth and free of dust before proceeding.

2. Priming: Depending on the type of protective coating being used, priming may be necessary to ensure proper adhesion and coverage. Primers help seal the wood and create a smooth base for the topcoat. They can be applied with a brush or spray gun and should be allowed to dry thoroughly before proceeding.

3. Coating Application: Once the surface is prepped and primed, the protective coating can be applied. Whether using shellac, polyurethane,

or lacquer, it's essential to follow the manufacturer's instructions for application and drying times. Thin, even coats should be applied, with ample drying time between each coat. Multiple coats may be necessary to achieve the desired level of protection and finish.

4. Finishing Touches: After the final coat has been applied and allowed to dry completely, any necessary finishing touches can be made. This may include sanding the surface with fine-grit sandpaper to remove any imperfections or unevenness. Once satisfied with the smoothness and appearance of the drum shell, it is ready for the next step in the drum-making process.

Applying protective coatings is a meticulous process that requires patience, attention to detail, and proper ventilation to ensure a professional-quality finish. By choosing the right type of coating and following the correct application techniques, drum makers can create instruments that not only sound great but also stand the test of time.

2. Installing Hardware (Rims, Lugs, and Tension Rods)

Installing hardware such as rims, lugs, and tension rods is a crucial aspect of drum making, as it directly impacts the drum's sound, playability, and overall aesthetic. These components work together to provide structural support, tuning capabilities, and a mounting system for drumheads. Proper installation ensures that the drum functions optimally and withstands the rigors of performance.

Types of Hardware

Rims: Drum rims, also known as hoops, are circular metal rings that hold the drumhead in place and provide tension for tuning. They come in various sizes and materials, including steel, chrome, and die-cast aluminum. Installing rims involves aligning them evenly around the drum shell and securing them with tension rods and lugs.

Lugs: Lugs are the metal casings attached to the drum shell that hold the tension rods in place. They come in different styles and designs, ranging from classic tube lugs to modern bridge lugs. Lugs play a critical role in distributing tension evenly across the drumhead, ensuring consistent tuning and resonance.

Tension Rods: Tension rods are threaded metal rods that pass through the lugs and connect to the rims. They are tightened or loosened to adjust the tension of the drumhead, thereby altering the pitch and tone of the drum. Tension rods typically have a square or hexagonal head for easy turning with a drum key.

Installation Process

1. Preparation: Before installing hardware, it is essential to mark the positions where the lugs and rims will be attached to the drum shell. This ensures even spacing and alignment for optimal performance. Additionally, any holes or mounting points should be drilled or prepped according to the hardware specifications.

2. Attaching Lugs: The first step in installing hardware is attaching the lugs to the drum shell. This is typically done using screws or bolts that secure the lug firmly in place. Lugs should be positioned evenly around the shell to distribute tension uniformly.

3. Mounting Rims: Once the lugs are installed, the rims can be mounted onto the drum shell. Rims are placed over the drumhead and aligned with the lugs, ensuring that each lug lines up with a corresponding hole in the rim. The rims are then secured in place using tension rods.

4. Inserting Tension Rods: With the rims in place, tension rods can be inserted through the lugs and threaded into the rim. It's important to ensure that each tension rod is inserted straight and evenly tightened to achieve consistent tension across the drumhead. A drum key is used to tighten or loosen the tension rods as needed.

5. Final Adjustments: Once all hardware is installed, a final check should be performed to ensure everything is securely in place and properly aligned. Tension rods may need to be adjusted slightly to achieve the desired drum tension and tone. Additionally, any excess hardware or protruding screws should be trimmed or filed down for a clean finish.

By following these steps, drum makers can effectively install hardware such as rims, lugs, and tension rods, ensuring that the drum is structurally sound and ready for tuning. Proper installation of hardware is essential for achieving optimal drum performance and sound quality.

3. Tuning the Drum

Tuning is perhaps one of the most critical aspects of drum making, as it directly affects the sound, tone, and playability of the instrument. Proper tuning ensures that the drum produces a clear, resonant sound and maintains a consistent pitch across all drumheads. Whether tuning a single drum or an entire drum set, it requires patience, practice, and an understanding of basic tuning principles.

Basic Tuning Principles

Tension: Drumheads are tensioned using tension rods and lugs to control the pitch and tone of the drum. Tightening the tension rods increases the pitch and produces a higher tone while loosening them lowers the pitch and creates a deeper tone.

It's essential to tune each drumhead evenly to maintain balance and resonance.

Resonance: Resonance refers to the ability of the drum to vibrate freely and produce a sustained sound. Proper tuning ensures that the drumhead resonates harmoniously with the drum shell, resulting in a clear, full-bodied sound. Adjusting the tension rods and tuning lugs helps achieve optimal resonance and sustain.

Balance: Balancing the tension between the top and bottom drumheads is crucial for achieving a well-rounded sound. Both drumheads should be tuned to the same pitch or tension to prevent unwanted overtones and ensure consistent tone and response. Tuning intervals may vary depending on the drum size, style, and musical preferences.

Tuning Process

1. Preparation: Before tuning the drum, it's essential to ensure that the drumhead is properly seated on the drum shell and free from any wrinkles or creases. This can be achieved by pressing down on the center of the drumhead and working outwards towards the edges. Additionally, make sure that all tension rods are securely in place and evenly tightened.

2. Tuning Sequence: Start by tuning the drum's resonant (bottom) head before moving on to the batter (top) head. This helps establish a solid foundation for tuning and ensures that the drum resonates evenly from both sides. Begin by tapping near each tension rod to identify any unevenness in pitch, then use a drum key to adjust the tension rods accordingly.

3. Even Tension: Work your way around the drum in a star or criss-cross pattern, gradually tightening each tension rod by a quarter turn at a time. This helps maintain even tension across the

drumhead and prevents warping or uneven stretching. Continue tuning each tension rod until the desired pitch is achieved, periodically tapping the drumhead to check for consistency.

4. Fine-Tuning: Once the drum is roughly tuned, fine-tune each tension rod to ensure precise pitch and tone. Make small adjustments as needed, tapping the drumhead and listening for any discrepancies in sound. Pay close attention to the drum's overall resonance and adjust accordingly to achieve optimal balance and sustain.

5. Repeat Process: Repeat the tuning process for the batter (top) head, following the same sequence and principles as the resonant head. Take your time to fine-tune each tension rod and listen carefully to the drum's sound, making adjustments as necessary to achieve uniformity and clarity.

By following these steps and principles, drum makers can effectively tune their drums to produce a clear, resonant sound that meets their musical preferences and performance needs. Practice and experimentation are key to mastering the art of tuning, allowing drum makers to unlock the full potential of their instruments and achieve professional-quality results.

CHAPTER FIVE

Playing And Maintenance

Learning Basic Drumming Techniques

Learning basic drumming techniques is essential for anyone interested in playing the drums effectively. Whether you're a beginner or looking to improve your skills, mastering these fundamentals lays a solid foundation for your musical journey.

Proper Grip and Stroke Technique

One of the first things to learn when starting out with drumming is how to hold the drumsticks correctly. The traditional grip involves holding the stick between your thumb and index finger with your other fingers wrapped around it. The match grip, on the other hand, involves holding both sticks in a similar manner, either with palms facing down or facing each other. Experiment with both grips to find what feels most comfortable for you.

Once you have your grip sorted, focus on your stroke technique. This includes understanding the difference between wrist strokes, finger strokes, and arm strokes. Wrist strokes are typically used for softer dynamics, while arm strokes generate more power for louder playing. Practice each stroke individually and then combine them to develop fluidity and control.

Basic Rhythms and Coordination Exercises

After mastering grip and stroke techniques, it's time to delve into basic rhythms and coordination exercises. Start with simple patterns like the single-stroke roll, double-stroke roll, and paradiddles. These patterns help improve coordination between your hands and build muscle memory.

As you progress, experiment with different time signatures and incorporate accents to add dynamics to your playing. Practice along with a metronome to improve your timing and keep yourself accountable. Consistent practice of these fundamental rhythms will enhance your drumming skills and prepare you for more complex patterns in the future.

Dynamics and Expression

Drumming isn't just about hitting things; it's about expressing yourself through rhythm and dynamics. Learning how to control the volume and intensity of your playing adds depth and emotion to your performances. Experiment with playing soft and loud strokes, and practice transitioning smoothly between different dynamic levels.

Additionally, explore techniques like ghost notes, accents, and buzz rolls to add texture and nuance to your playing. Understanding dynamics allows you to convey emotion and musicality, making your drumming more engaging and expressive.

Caring for Your Handcrafted Drum

Proper care and maintenance are crucial for preserving the quality and longevity of your handcrafted drum. Whether you've purchased a drum or crafted one yourself, following these guidelines will ensure it stays in optimal condition for years to come.

Storage and Transportation

When not in use, store your drum in a cool, dry place away from direct sunlight and extreme temperatures. Avoid storing it in areas prone to humidity or moisture, as this can damage the drum's materials over time. If transporting your drum, use a padded case or bag to protect it from bumps and scratches.

Cleaning and Polishing

Regular cleaning is essential to remove dirt, dust, and sweat buildup from your drum's surface. Use a soft, lint-free cloth to gently wipe down the drum after each use. For stubborn stains or residue, lightly dampen the cloth with water or a mild soap solution. Avoid using harsh chemicals or abrasive cleaners, as they can damage the drum's finish.

Periodically, apply a drum-specific polish or wax to maintain the drum's shine and protect its surface. Be sure to follow the manufacturer's instructions and test the product on a small, inconspicuous area before applying it to the entire drum.

Tuning and Maintenance

Keeping your drum properly tuned is essential for achieving the best sound quality and performance. Invest in a quality drum key and learn how to tune each drumhead to your desired pitch. Regularly check for loose tension rods or damaged drumheads, and make adjustments as needed to ensure optimal tension and resonance.

Inspect the drum's hardware, including lugs, hoops, and tension rods, for any signs of wear or damage. Replace any worn or damaged parts promptly to prevent further issues and maintain the drum's structural integrity.

Troubleshooting Common Issues

Even with proper care and maintenance, drums can encounter issues from time to time. Knowing how to troubleshoot common problems will help you address issues quickly and effectively, ensuring uninterrupted playability.

Drumhead Damage or Wear

One of the most common issues drummers face is damage or wear to the drumheads. Over time, drumheads can become stretched, dented, or torn, affecting the drum's sound and performance. If you notice any signs of damage, such as wrinkles, punctures, or uneven tension, it's time to replace the drumhead.

To replace a drumhead, first, remove the old head and clean the bearing edge and hoop. Place the new head evenly over the drum shell, ensuring it sits flat and centered. Tighten the tension rods gradually in a crisscross pattern to achieve uniform tension and prevent warping.

Loose Hardware or Rattles

Another common issue is loose hardware or rattles, which can detract from the drum's sound quality and performance. Inspect the drum's hardware, including tension rods, lugs, and mounting brackets, for any signs of looseness or damage. Tighten any loose hardware using a drum key, taking care not to over-tighten and strip the threads.

If you're still experiencing rattling noises, check for any loose accessories or objects inside the drum shell, such as stray screws, washers, or debris. Remove any foreign objects and reassemble the drum, ensuring all components are securely in place.

Uneven Sound or Tuning

Uneven sound or tuning issues can occur if the drumheads are not properly tensioned or if there are discrepancies in the drum's construction. Use a drum key to set the tension rods evenly around the drumhead, making minor changes until you attain a constant pitch and tone.

If the drum still sounds uneven or out of tune, examine the drum's bearing edges for any imperfections or damage. Uneven bearing edges can cause the drumhead to sit unevenly, diminishing its overall sound quality. In such instances, seek a skilled drum mechanic for repair or reconditioning.

Summary

As you complete your drum manufacturing adventure, take a minute to think about the great experience you've had. From selecting the appropriate materials to manufacturing each component with care and accuracy, you've put your heart and soul into creating something incredibly exceptional. Whether you're a seasoned craftsman or a newbie artisan, the process of constructing a drum from scratch is a tremendously satisfying one that develops creativity, patience, and a connection to both tradition and innovation.

Reflecting on Your Drum-Making Journey

As you reflect back on the steps you've taken and the problems you've conquered, analyze how your talents have changed along the process. Perhaps you met difficulties along the road, such as obtaining hard-to-find materials or learning complicated procedures, but each hurdle only served to reinforce your drive and enhance your grasp of the trade. Take satisfaction in the knowledge that every part of your drum, from the choice of wood to the tuning of the head, carries the mark of your commitment and ability.

Reflect also on the cultural significance of the drum, which has been a vital aspect of human expression for millennia. Across countries and continents, drums have functioned as instruments of communication, celebration, and spiritual connection, overcoming language barriers to join people in rhythm and harmony. By engaging in the age-old tradition of drum building, you've become part of this rich tapestry of human experience, giving your own unique contribution to its continuous growth.

Consider, too, the personal meaning of your drum manufacturing adventure. Perhaps you took on this venture as a form of self-expression, seeking a creative outlet for your hobbies and abilities. Or maybe you were drawn to the contemplative character of working with your hands, finding consolation and joy in the rhythmic repetition of each activity. Whatever the motive, take a minute to recognize the ways in which this event has enhanced your life and enlarged your perspectives.

 Finally, as you stare upon the completed product of your labor—a beautiful, one-of-a-kind drum that vibrates with the spirit of your craftsmanship—let yourself experience a feeling of success and happiness. Know that you have not only made a musical instrument of enduring beauty and quality but also formed a closer link to the ancient art of drum manufacturing and the global network of artists who share your passion.

Further Resources For Drum-Making Enthusiasts

While your drum manufacturing adventure may be coming to an end, your investigation of this fascinating skill is far from done. Fortunately, there are a variety of tools available to assist you continue polishing your talents and broadening your awareness of drum-building techniques and traditions.

Books: With a range of educational books and manuals delve into the rich history and many skills of drum building. There's no shortage of reading material to inspire and enrich your practice, from extensive manuals that cover everything from material selection to final instrument tuning, to coffee table books that highlight the incredible workmanship of professional drum builders worldwide.

Online Communities: Through social media groups, specialized websites, and online forums, get in touch with other drum manufacturing lovers and professionals. Talk about your personal experiences, ask for guidance and criticism, and absorb the knowledge of those who have made comparable mistakes. These online forums are a great place to discuss your newest project or ask for troubleshooting advice; they are also a great source of information and assistance.

Workshops and seminars: With practical workshops and seminars taught by seasoned drum makers and craftspeople, you may advance your talents to the next level. Whether you'd rather learn in-person or digitally, there are many of options to become fully immersed in the field and receive knowledgeable, hands-on instruction. Everything for every interest and ability level is available, from introductory sessions for beginners to expert masterclasses.

Materials and providers: To inspire your creativity and experimentation, investigate a variety of materials and providers. You have a plethora of alternatives to help you realize your idea, whether you're looking for specialist hardware and accessories, high-quality drum heads, or wood that has been obtained responsibly. Spend some time investigating several vendors and materials to determine which one best suits your requirements and price range.

In summary, your road toward drum creation is a lifetime quest for expertise and self-discovery rather than a single endeavor. You'll improve your drum-making abilities and enhance your life in many ways by thinking back on your experiences, looking for new materials, and just exploring and experimenting. Thus, never stop producing, drumming, and maintaining the beat.

THE END